COPING WITH POPULATION GROWTH

Nicola Barber

Chicago, Illinois

www.heinemannraintree.com
Visit our website to find out more information about Heinemann-Raintree books.

To order:
☎ Phone 888-454-2279
💻 Visit www.heinemannraintree.com to browse our catalog and order online.

Edited by Andrew Farrow and Adam Miller
Designed by Victoria Allen
Original illustrations © Capstone Global Library Ltd.
Illustrated by Tower Designs UK Limited
Picture research by Mica Brancic
Production by Camilla Crask
Originated by Capstone Global Library Ltd.
Printed and bound in China by South China Printing Company.

15 14 13 12 11
10 9 8 7 6 5 4 3 2 1

Library of Congress Cataloging-in-Publication Data
Barber, Nicola.
  Coping with population growth / Nicola Barber.
    p. cm.—(The environment challenge)
  Includes bibliographical references and index.
  ISBN 978-1-4109-4296-8 (hb freestyle)—ISBN 978-1-4109-4303-3 (pb freestyle) 1. Population—Juvenile literature. 2. Population—Environmental aspects—Juvenile literature. I. Title.
  HB883.B37 2012
  304.6'2—dc22   2010052702

ISBNs: 978-1-4109-4296-8 (HC); 978-1-4109-4303-3 (PB)

Acknowledgments
The author and publishers are grateful to the following for permission to reproduce copyright material: Corbis p. 5 © Danny Lehman, p. 6 AgStock Image/© Rick Dalton, p. 8 epa/© Jagadeesh NV, p. 9 epa/© Nic Bothma, p. 10 © Wendy Stone, p. 13 Reuters/© Rafiqur Rahman, p. 18 National Geographic Society/© Tyrone Turner, p. 22 Asia Images/© Wang Leng, p. 28 Xinhua Press/XinHua/© Liu Quanlong, p. 35 © Carlos Cazalis, p. 36 © Frans Lanting, p. 37 JAI/© Michele Falzone, p. 38 Blend Images/© Jetta Productions; Getty Images p. 11 Sean Gallup, p. 14 AFP PHOTO/Noah Seelam, p. 21 Bloomberg/Jamie Rector, p. 24 Time Life Pictures/Robert Nickelsberg, p. 25 Brent Stirton, p. 27 AFP Photo/Roberto SchmidtT, p. 32 Photodisc, p. 39 Jeff J Mitchell , p. 40 AFP Photo/A Majeed; Reuters p. 41 © Todd Korol; Shutterstock p. 34 © Pawel Pietraszewski.

Cover photograph of a nurse checking the temperature of babies at a maternity ward in a hospital in Manila used with permission of Reuters/© Cheryl Ravelo.

We would like to thank Michael D. Mastrandrea, Ph.D. for his invaluable help in the preparation of this book.

Every effort has been made to contact copyright holders of any material reproduced in this book. Any omissions will be rectified in subsequent printings if notice is given to the publisher.

Disclaimer
All the Internet addresses (URLs) given in this book were valid at the time of going to press. However, due to the dynamic nature of the Internet, some addresses may have changed, or sites may have changed or ceased to exist since publication. While the author and publisher regret any inconvenience this may cause readers, no responsibility for any such changes can be accepted by either the author or the publisher.

Contents

Words appearing in the text in bold, **like this**, are explained in the glossary.

Counting the World's Population

"If we don't halt population growth with justice and compassion, it will be done for us by nature, brutally and without pity—and will leave a ravaged world."

Dr. Henry W. Kendall, Nobel Prize winner

Natural increase

Dr. Kendall's words highlight the importance of population growth for everyone on our planet. In 2009 there were 264 babies born every minute across the world. In the same year, there were 107 deaths every minute. Subtract the number of people dying from the number of people being born, and you will see that the world's population increased by 157 people every minute in 2009.

This **"natural increase"** (the difference between births and deaths) may not at first seem very impressive—that is, until you start to add it up. Every hour in 2009, the world's population increased by around 9,420 people. Every day, it increased by approximately 226,000 people. Over the whole year, the 2009 figure for natural increase was nearly 83 million people.

Looking back in time

If we look back in time, it is clear that the world's population has not always grown at such a rate. Around 2,000 years ago, it is estimated that there were about 300 million people living on Earth. It took another 1,600 years for this figure to double to 600 million. Up until the 1900s, the world's population grew relatively slowly, reaching 1 billion in 1804 and 1.7 billion by 1900.

Examining the evidence

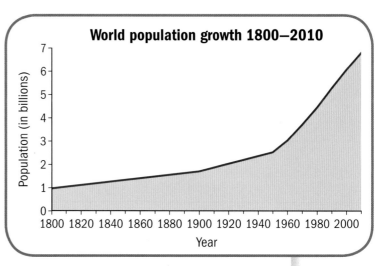

Year	Population (in billions)
1804	1.0
1900	1.7
1950	2.52
1960	3.02
1970	3.70
1980	4.44
1990	5.27
2000	6.06
2010	6.79

World population growth 1800–2010

A table is useful for presenting raw **data** (a collection of facts). But convert this table into a simple graph (right), and you get an even clearer picture of the sudden steep growth in population after 1950.

World population

The explosion of world population growth began after 1950. Look at the figures in the table and graph on the previous page. By 1960 the number of people on Earth had reached 3 billion. It took only 14 years to reach 4 billion (in 1974), a mere 13 years to hit 5 billion (in 1987), and another 13 years to top 6 billion (by the year 2000).

Population growth and the environment

This rapid growth in population has put massive pressure on Earth and its resources. In this book, we look at the reasons for the population explosion, as well as what is likely to happen in the future. We will examine how the number of people living on our planet is linked to the environmental challenges that we face. And we will learn how people are tackling population growth across the world.

Many cities around the world have areas of slums or **shantytowns** where millions of people live, often without access to basic services such as water and sanitation. This shanty town is in São Paulo, Brazil.

WORD BANK
data — collection of facts
natural increase — difference between the number of births and deaths in a particular place

5

Population growth: Good or bad?

For many years, people have disagreed about exactly how many people our planet can support. They also disagree about whether there are too many people in the world. These arguments started over 200 years ago, when an English **economist** (person who studies money) named Thomas Malthus said that populations would always grow faster than the food supply. He argued that this would result in war, famine (extreme food shortages), and disease.

Since that time, economists and demographers (people who study populations) have continued to debate the pros and cons of population growth. Many think that environmental issues, such as the destruction of the world's forests, are directly linked to overpopulation. They say that too many people are putting too much pressure on Earth's limited resources. Others have argued that the population explosion is balanced out by human inventiveness. They say that people will always come up with new ideas and technologies that will allow humans to survive.

These combine harvesters are at work in vast fields of barley in Washington state. The industrialization of farming is one example of a technology that supports the world's growing population.

Population slow-down?

In fact, many experts think that the world's population growth will slow down during the 2000s. They say that better education about **family planning** will allow parents to choose to have fewer children. The **United Nations (UN)** has predicted that the world's population will be around 8 billion by 2025 and 9 billion by 2050 —a much slower rate of growth than has been experienced since the 1950s.

Examining the evidence

If you need population statistics for your research, there are several good websites you could look at. The advantage of using the Internet for this kind of information is that good websites will keep their statistics up-to-date.

- The most reliable source for information about populations is the UN. For access to lots of data, go to www.un.org/popin/.

- To search for population statistics for many countries and regions of the world, look at this UN link: http://esa.un.org/unpp/index.asp?panel=1.

- Other websites base their information on statistics taken from the UN and other sources. The following useful website uses both the UN and the U.S. **Census** Bureau (see pages 8 and 9) to feed its real-time population count: www.worldometers.info/.

Natural increase (see page 4) is expressed here as a number per 1,000. So, a figure of 17.8 means that for every 1,000 people, the population increased by another 17.8 people during the relevant period (10 years in this example).

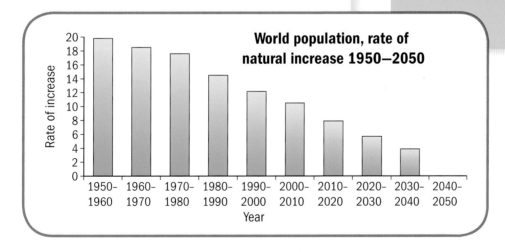

World population, rate of natural increase 1950—2050

Collecting the data

In order to understand populations, it is essential for governments and world organizations like the UN to have accurate information.

In most countries, population data is collected by doing a census. At its most basic, this is a count of everyone living and working in a particular country at a particular time. But in addition to collecting raw data, census workers also usually gather information such as how old people are, where they live, and what work they do. All of this information is important for governments as they plan for services such as housing, health, and education.

Census problems

Since censuses are very expensive to operate, most countries hold them only every 10 years. Some poor countries simply cannot afford to have a census. For these countries, estimates have to be made about their populations.

There are many issues that can affect a census. The size and landscape of a country can make it difficult to reach all of the people. Some countries may have climates that make it difficult to reach parts of the population at certain times of the year.

A country at war is unlikely to be able to hold a census. In addition, people are often forced to move during times of war, which affects the accuracy of the count. These people, called **refugees**, may spend months or years in another country because it is not safe to return to their homes.

An Indian census official records information about family members who live in one of the slum areas of Bangalore, in southern India.

The U.S. Census

In the United States, a census is held every 10 years. For the most recent, in 2010, a form containing 10 questions was mailed out to every address in the country. Anyone who did not return the form got a visit from a census-taker, who asked the same 10 questions. Information from the census was used to give out around $400 billion of government money to states. This information also helped to determine how different areas were represented in the U.S. Congress.

However, in 2010 there were up to 12 million people in the United States who had entered the country illegally. The U.S. Census Bureau cannot by law share the information it receives with anyone. But many people may still have avoided filling out a census form because they did not want to reveal that they were in the country illegally. Because of this, the final count is perhaps not totally accurate.

Refugees wait at a food and clothing distribution point at a camp in Sudan. These people have been forced to move from their homes because of civil war in their country. War, and the movement of large numbers of people, make it almost impossible to hold a census.

WORD BANK
refugee   person who is forced to leave his or her home as a result of war or natural disaster

More and More People

Why has the world's population grown so dramatically since the 1950s? The main reason is that, in general, people are healthier. As a result, they are living longer. Developments in medicine have meant that many diseases that were once killers can now be either prevented or treated. Some diseases, such as smallpox, have disappeared entirely (see the box at right), saving thousands, if not millions, of lives. Antibiotic drugs, such as penicillin, have also revolutionized the treatment of infections and many illnesses.

Water and sanitation

Alongside developments in modern medicine, many people in **developed countries**, meaning wealthier countries like the United States and the United Kingdom, have benefited from access to clean water supplies and modern systems that treat **sewage**. In the past, diseases such as cholera and typhus quickly spread through dirty water. Today, many people can take it for granted that the water that comes out of their faucets is clean and safe to drink.

But in many poorer countries, called **developing countries**, this is not the case. In slum housing or **refugee** camps, there are often no systems to provide clean water or to remove sewage. As a result, diseases such as cholera remain a huge risk. The World Health Organization estimates that between 100,000 and 300,000 people continue to die every year as a result of cholera outbreaks. (See pages 30 and 31 for more about the world's water.)

These children in a slum in Nairobi, Kenya, are playing in an open sewer. Outbreaks of cholera are frequent in this and other slums in Nairobi because of the lack of **sanitation**.

The smallpox story

Smallpox is a horrific disease that has spread across the world throughout history, killing thousands of people at a time. In the past, an outbreak of the disease left about one-third of its victims dead, and many survivors were blinded and terribly scarred. Despite developments in **vaccinations**, which helped to prevent the disease, it is estimated that smallpox was the cause of between 300 million and 500 million deaths in the 1900s alone.

In 1967 the World Health Organization launched a plan to end smallpox completely through worldwide vaccination campaigns. This amazing milestone was achieved in the late 1970s.

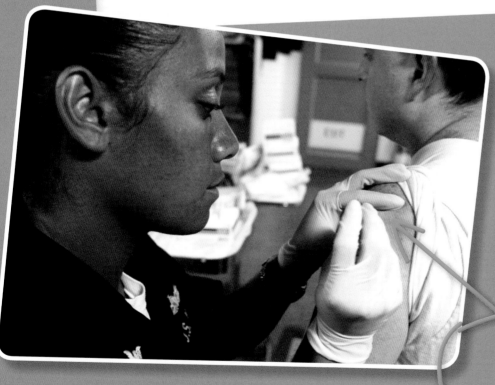

A nurse gives a smallpox vaccine. The use of this vaccine has helped to wipe out the disease across the world.

WORD BANK

developed country	wealthy country where people have a high standard of living
developing country	poor country where people do not have a high standard of living
sewage	dirty water from toilets, baths, and sinks
vaccination	technique of giving a person a tiny amount of a disease (the vaccine) to give the person protection against the disease in the future

Life expectancy

In general, people can expect to live longer today than they would have in the past. In the United States, **life expectancy** (the average life span) for babies born in 1900 was 48 years. In 2010 it was estimated at over 78 years. Today, life expectancy in most developed countries is around 80 years.

In many developing countries, however, life expectancy remains much lower. For example, in Afghanistan the life expectancy for men and women is 44 years.

Uneven population growth

Although the world's population continues to grow, this growth is very unevenly distributed around the world. In many developed countries, population growth has stabilized or even stopped. In some developed countries, populations are remaining stable only because of **migration** (the movement of people) into those countries (see page 39).

High living standards and widespread health care services in developed countries have allowed women to choose to have fewer babies. Women in developed countries also tend to marry and have their children later than people in most developing countries.

Today, the world's population growth is taking place in developing countries. For the period 2005 to 2010, the average number of children per woman in Europe was 1.5, while in Africa it was 4.6. Poor health care services in many developing countries make it difficult for women to get **family planning** services. In many places, women cannot get hold of **contraceptives** in order to stop unwanted pregnancies. Women also tend to marry and have their children earlier than people in developed countries.

This chart compares the population growth rate of more developed countries (MDCs) and less developed countries (LDCs). The worldwide growth rate is slowing in both developed countries and developing countries. But population growth is now centered in developing countries.

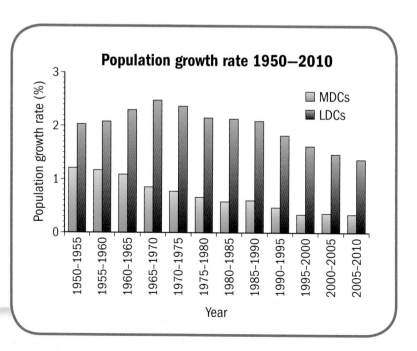

Bangladesh

Bangladesh, in South Asia, has a population of around 156 million people. About 19 percent of this population is between the ages of 15 and 24 years old. Girls tend to marry very early in Bangladesh—about half before they are 18 years old. A large proportion of women become pregnant or have their first child before they are 20.

Marriage at a young age, when women are very **fertile** (capable of becoming pregnant), contributed to Bangladesh's massive surge in population in the 1960s and 1970s. Since then the rate of population growth has slowed, as more women have been able to use contraception. Nevertheless, Bangladesh still has a high rate of births to women under the age of 20.

Parents and children in Dhaka, Bangladesh.

WORD BANK

contraceptive	device or drug that is used to prevent pregnancy
fertile	capable of reproducing
life expectancy	average number of years people from a certain place live
migration	movement of people

What would YOU do ?

The theme for the World Population Day in 2010 was "Everyone Counts." Every year, the UNFPA tries to raise awareness of population issues by using posters, sporting events, concerts, and other celebrations. What other themes would you choose? How would you get people really thinking about the issues?

How many children?

The high birth rates in developing countries are not always by choice. The **United Nations** Population Fund (UNFPA) estimates that across the world, there are 200 million women who would like to control their pregnancies, but are unable to do so.

The mission statement of the UNFPA states that it supports countries "in using population **data** for policies and programs to reduce poverty and to ensure that every pregnancy is wanted." Every year on July 11, the UNFPA holds a World Population Day. On this day, the group highlights the fact that it is a basic human right to be able to decide how many children to have, and when to have them. It is hoped that such programs will help control the rate of population growth in developing countries.

Nurses in Hyderabad, India, take part in a parade to celebrate World Population Day on July 11, 2010.

Aging populations

A major reason for increased population figures in developed countries is older people. Thanks to increasing life expectancy rates (see page 12), some countries have a much higher proportion of older people in their populations than ever before.

For example, the United States has one of the highest proportions of older people in the world. The number of people over 65 years old was 35 million in 2000. It is estimated that this will rise to 71 million in 2030.

This aging population is bringing new challenges. For example, many developed countries are already spending more money on pensions (money paid regularly to retired people) and on health care for the elderly.

Young populations

In contrast, many developing countries have relatively young populations. In Africa, for example, people between the ages of 15 and 24 made up 9 percent of the population in 1950. By 2050 this percentage is predicted to grow to 29 percent.

This increase in the young population also brings new challenges for the future. Countries will need to provide services like education, health care, and jobs for this youthful population. Gaps in employment will be left when aging populations in developed countries retire. This gap will increasingly be filled by people from developing countries, encouraging more migration (see page 39).

Population pyramids

A population pyramid is a useful tool to help you analyze the population structure of a country. The pyramid shows the population of a country, broken down into age groups. The information covers five-year age spans (0 to 4, 5 to 9, 10 to 14, and so on, as shown on pages 16 and 17). It is broken down into male and female categories. The number of males is shown on the left-hand side of the pyramid, while the number of females is shown on the right.

There are two shapes that are typical population pyramids. The first (A), which is common for developing countries, has a broad bottom and a narrow top. The second (B), which is common for developed countries, is a broader, bulging shape.

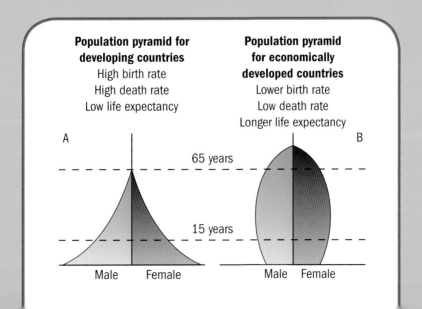

Population pyramid for developing countries
High birth rate
High death rate
Low life expectancy

Population pyramid for economically developed countries
Lower birth rate
Low death rate
Longer life expectancy

A

65 years

15 years

B

Male   Female

Male   Female

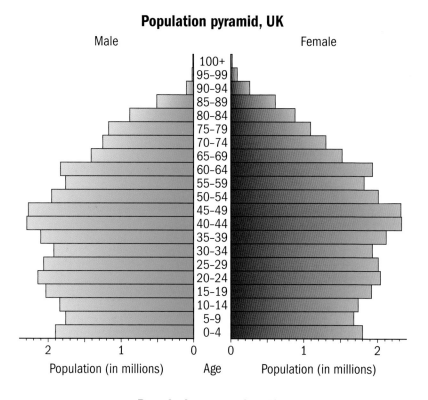

Population pyramid, UK

Male — Female

Population (in millions) — Age — Population (in millions)

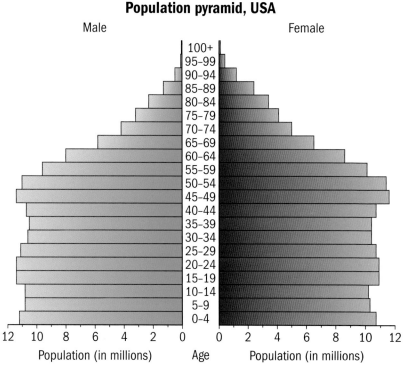

Population pyramid, USA

Male — Female

Population (in millions) — Age — Population (in millions)

In 2010, the population pyramids for the United States and the United Kingdom looked like this. As you can see, their shape is very similar. How do they compare to the pyramids on page 15?

You can make a population pyramid for any country in the world. The raw data is available from the UN's website at http://esa.un.org/unpp/index.asp?panel=2. Under "Select variables," select "Population by five-year age group and sex," then select your required country, and then choose a start year and end year. The numbers are given in thousands, so you need to add three zeroes to get the real number (for example, 5,919 means 5,919,000).

Niger, The story behind the statistics

Niger, in West Africa, lies on the edge of the Sahara Desert. It has a population of more than 15 million people and an average life expectancy of 53 years. It has a low rate of **literacy** (the number of people who can read and write) and high rates of disease. The country often suffers from **droughts** (long periods with no rain) that devastate livestock and crops.

In 2009 a serious drought led to crops not growing in Niger. As a result, the price of the foods that were available to buy soared. Most people could not afford even the most basic supplies. Thousands of people were forced to leave their homes and travel hundreds of miles in search of food. Others had to rely on emergency food aid. (See page 27 for more about food aid and food supplies.)

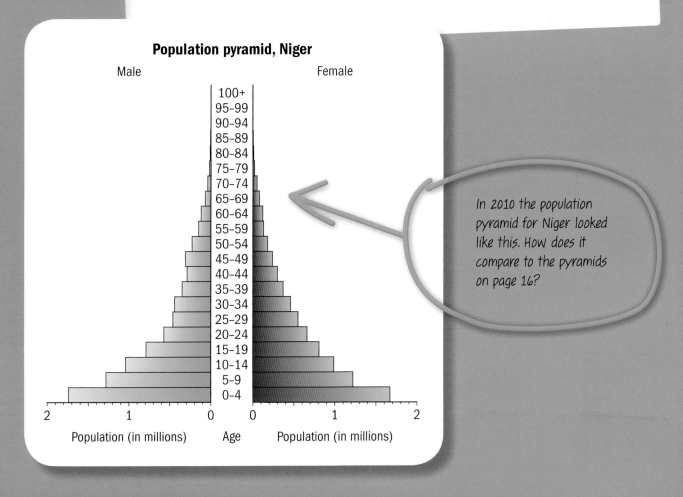

Population pyramid, Niger

In 2010 the population pyramid for Niger looked like this. How does it compare to the pyramids on page 16?

WORD BANK
drought   long period without rain
literacy   ability to read and write

Global Footprints

The billions of people who live on our planet have a massive impact on its resources. We rely on our planet for the water we drink, the food we eat, and the energy we consume in our homes.

What would YOU do ?

How could you reduce the size of your own ecological footprint? Begin by thinking about the factors that affect your footprint. They include choices such as whether you buy local or imported food and other goods, what kind of transportation you use, and whether you recycle. You can assess your ecological footprint on the website of the Global Footprint Network at www.footprintnetwork.org/en/index.php/GFN/page/calculators/.

The impact of each person on the planet's resources is known as an **ecological footprint**, or **global footprint**. This measurement can also be applied to countries. The ecological footprint measures how fast we consume resources and generate waste, compared to how fast Earth can absorb our waste and generate new resources. Overall, it has been calculated that humans today use the equivalent of 1.5 planets to provide the resources we need, and to absorb the waste we produce. In other words, we are using resources faster than the planet can create them.

These people have put their waste into special boxes for recycling. One way to reduce our ecological impact is to reduce the amount of garbage that we throw away.

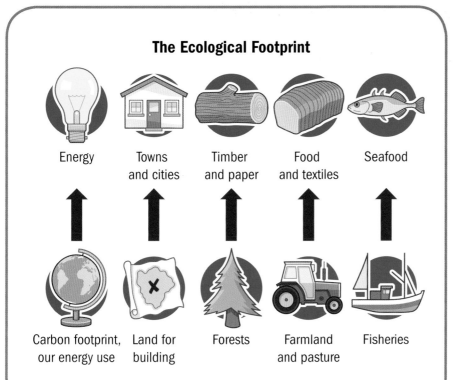

The Ecological Footprint

Energy	Towns and cities	Timber and paper	Food and textiles	Seafood
↑	↑	↑	↑	↑
Carbon footprint, our energy use	Land for building	Forests	Farmland and pasture	Fisheries

The ecological footprint measures our consumption of Earth's resources and how much waste we create, compared to how much nature can provide new resources and absorb waste. The demands that humans place on our planet have increased as a result of the population explosion and individual **consumption** (buying and using things).

Ecological footprints

The two countries with the largest ecological footprints in 2005 were the United States and China. But compare the ecological footprint per person in each country. China's population in 2005 was 1.3 billion, compared to just over 300 million people in the United States. This means that the per-person ecological footprint in the United States is much larger than that of a Chinese citizen. In fact, if every person in the world lived like the average person in the United States, we would need 4.5 Earths to survive.

India had the next-largest overall footprint in 2005. But if every person in the world lived like the average person in India, we would need less than half of the world's resources to survive. **Developed countries** consume about 80 percent of the world's resources, although they make up only about 20 percent of its population.

In the early 1960s, most countries were able to meet the needs of their populations. But today, this situation has changed completely. Many countries now rely on **importing** resources such as food, fuel, and even water from other parts of the world in order to meet demand.

A sustainable future?

How can we work toward a future in which everyone on Earth has a fair share of the planet's resources? There are two main challenges: reducing consumption and controlling population growth.

Tackling consumption

In developed countries, population growth is low, but consumption per person is high. The challenge is to persuade people to consume fewer resources and produce less waste and **pollution**. Pollution is harm to the environment caused by waste and unnatural substances, such as car exhaust.

Nonrenewable resources

A major issue of consumption is our reliance on oil, coal, and natural gas, all of which are **nonrenewable** resources. This means that once supplies of these resources are used up, they cannot be replaced. We burn oil, coal, and natural gas to create the energy needed to make electricity, to fuel our cars, and to heat our homes.

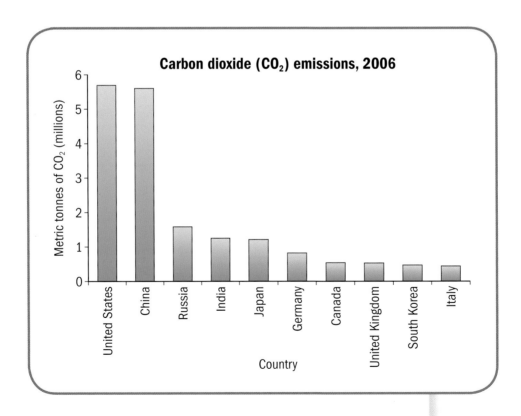

In 2006, the United States and China had the highest CO_2 emissions in the world.

A side effect of burning nonrenewable fuel sources like oil, coal, and natural gas is the production of the gas **carbon dioxide** (CO_2). Carbon dioxide is known as a greenhouse gas. This is because it traps heat from the Sun in the envelope of gases that surround Earth, in the same way that a greenhouse holds in heat. It is widely believed that higher levels of carbon dioxide and other greenhouse gases have led to an increase in global temperatures, known as **global warming**.

Unequal pollution

The problem of global warming is closely linked to population issues. You can see from the chart on page 20 that most carbon dioxide **emissions** come from developed countries. Yet it is people in **developing countries** who are most vulnerable to the consequences of emissions (see page 22).

Note also that China and India, which are quickly developing new businesses and factories, are producing a lot of carbon dioxide (see the box below). As other countries similarly develop, and their standards of living rise, so too will their carbon dioxide emissions—unless new and cleaner technologies are developed quickly. Slowing down the rate of population growth in these countries will create more time to put these measures into place.

Countries with the highest carbon dioxide (CO_2) emissions, 2006

Country	Metric tonnes of CO_2 (millions)
United States	5,697
China	5,607
Russia	1,587
India	1,250
Japan	1,213
Germany	823
Canada	539
United Kingdom	536
South Korea	476
Italy	448

Renewable resources

Renewable sources of energy provide an alternative to nonrenewable sources. They include solar (Sun) power, wind power, and wave and tide power. These developing technologies are essential as we find ways to reduce our dependence on coal, oil, and natural gas. They are also much "cleaner" sources of energy.

WORD BANK

emission	release of a gas
global warming	worldwide rise in the surface temperature of Earth
nonrenewable	something that cannot be replaced once it runs out
renewable	something that can be replaced naturally, and therefore cannot run out

Tackling population growth

According to a **UN** report in 2009, controlling population growth lies at the heart of dealing with global warming and the **climate change** (change in weather patterns) that it causes. As this report explains, the parts of the world with the highest rates of population growth are hit the hardest by the results of climate change. These results include flooding caused by rising sea levels, **drought** and failed crops, and the spread of disease.

Still, the global situation would be much worse if countries such as China and India had not already taken drastic measures to slow down their population growth. Governments in both of these countries have used policies and laws to force people to have fewer children.

In India during the 1970s, many people were either paid or forced to be sterilized, meaning they had an operation that prevented them from having babies. In 1979 China introduced its "one-child policy," which limited most families to having just one baby. Although these policies were effective in reducing population growth, many people criticized them for being unfair, because they denied people's basic right to choose for themselves.

A typical Chinese one-child family. Today the one-child-only policy applies mainly in Chinese cities.

"Little emperors"

In 2007 Chinese government officials claimed that the country's one-child policy had prevented more than 400 million births since its introduction in 1979.

In fact, the policy applies mainly in cities. Families living in **rural** (countryside) areas may be allowed two children, especially if the first child is a girl. Chinese tradition favors sons over daughters, as many parents want a son to care for them when they are older. It is thought that for some people this preference is so strong that they have allowed girl babies to die in order to be able to try again for a boy.

Certainly there are now more men than women in China—for every 100 women there are approximately 120 men. Because of this imbalance, Chinese officials have estimated that by 2020 there will be millions of Chinese "bare branches," meaning men unable to find wives. Many of these single children are also finding themselves burdened with caring for two parents and four grandparents.

The one-child policy has had some unexpected consequences. A generation of children have grown up without brothers and sisters, and have become used to the complete attention of doting parents. For this reason, these only children are known as "little emperors." There are concerns that the one-child policy has affected the behavior of millions of children.

Today, the birth rate in China has fallen to around 1.8 children per woman. This is below the rate (2.1 children) that would keep the population stable. This number of births is called the **replacement level**. Even if the Chinese government decides to relax the policy, it seems that people in China may have become used to having smaller families. Many Chinese couples in **urban** (city) areas are reluctant to have more than one child because they want to maintain their rising standard of living.

WORD BANK

climate change	change in the temperature, rainfall, or wind of a region
replacement level	number of births that will keep the population stable from one generation to the next
rural	from the countryside
urban	from the city

Effective family planning

Today, most governments and experts agree that the most effective way to control population growth is not by force, but rather by giving people the information and support they need to make their own choices. This means setting up **family planning** clinics where women and their partners can receive advice about **contraceptives**. It also means that people need reliable access to supplies of contraceptives. As you will see from the case study opposite, this is not always easy in remote, rural areas.

A health worker at a mobile family planning clinic in Pakistan explains contraceptive choices to local women.

An unwanted pregnancy

In Kenya, in Africa, a mother of six is expecting another child—but she does not want to be. She knows exactly what she needed to do to avoid another pregnancy, but her local health care center kept running out of contraceptives. Before new supplies could arrive, she was pregnant once again. She lives in a rural community, far from the nearest city. She finds it hard to feed and clothe the children she already has, and she cannot afford for them to go to school.

This is the reality of family planning in many developing countries. Kenya has an average of 4.6 births per woman. In the past, priority has been given to projects aimed at fighting the spread of **HIV/AIDS**. But the government in Kenya is now planning a boost for family planning projects. Dr. Boniface K'Oyugi, the head of the government agency in charge of population issues, said recently: "We must invest in population programs if we are to guarantee a good future for our people."

These children are having a lesson at an outdoor school in Kenya. Education is often the first casualty if parents have little money to spend on their children.

WORD BANK
HIV/AIDS   Human Immunodeficiency Virus (HIV) is a virus that attacks the body's immune system. Acquired Immune Deficiency Syndrome (AIDS) is caused by HIV.

25

Food and Water

In 2009 more than one billion people in the world did not have enough to eat. The number of hungry people has been increasing over recent years, yet worldwide there is enough food to go around. Most people in **developed countries** have enough to eat, and obesity (being very overweight) is an increasing problem in many Western countries.

Food insecurity

Across the world, most **fertile** land is already being used. As populations have grown, people have increasingly been forced onto land with poor soil or too little rainfall. In other places, the need to grow more food for larger families has meant that fertile land is overused.

Many countries cannot grow enough food to supply their own populations. So, to make up the shortfall, they buy and **import** food from elsewhere. This makes them vulnerable to changes in the price of food on the global markets. If the price of food goes up worldwide, people have to pay more for this imported food at their local markets or stores.

For people in many **developing countries**, even a small rise in prices can cause terrible hardship. Most people are hungry not because there is no food, but because they cannot afford to buy the food they need.

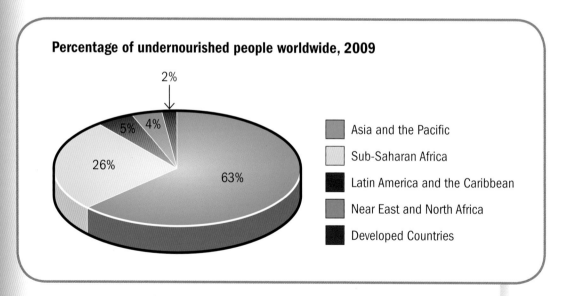

Percentage of undernourished people worldwide, 2009

2%
5% 4%
26%
63%

- Asia and the Pacific
- Sub-Saharan Africa
- Latin America and the Caribbean
- Near East and North Africa
- Developed Countries

It is estimated that 1.02 billion people were undernourished in 2009. The majority of these people were in Asia and the Pacific (63%), and sub-Saharan Africa (26%). Hunger mainly results from high food prices, lower incomes, and increasing unemployment.

People crowd around a truck delivering food aid in a slum in Nairobi. Sometimes food aid to hungry people is transported very long distances from wealthier countries.

Food aid

The first response when people in poorer countries are suffering from lack of food is often to send aid.

But many food experts say that such aid is unnecessary and often unhelpful, except in the direst of emergencies. They point out that food is usually available locally, but that the prices may be too high for most people to afford. Giving people small amounts of cash or vouchers allows them to buy the food they need until the next harvest, or until their situation changes.

Moreover, flooding local markets with food aid has long-term effects. It often forces down the price of food, which means that local farmers suffer because they cannot make a living from selling their own produce.

A concept web can be used to show the relationship between food, supplies, poverty, and population.

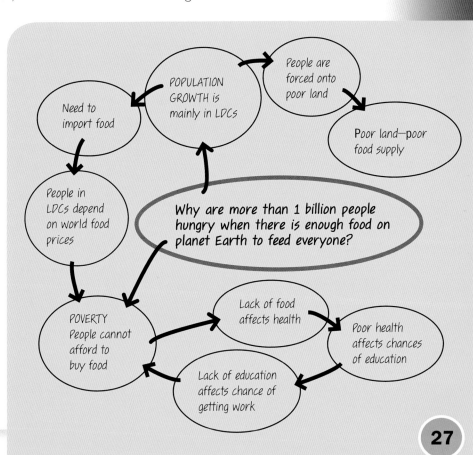

Need to import food

POPULATION GROWTH is mainly in LDCs

People are forced onto poor land

Poor land—poor food supply

People in LDCs depend on world food prices

Why are more than 1 billion people hungry when there is enough food on planet Earth to feed everyone?

POVERTY People cannot afford to buy food

Lack of food affects health

Poor health affects chances of education

Lack of education affects chance of getting work

27

Long-term thinking

To help people in developing countries protect themselves against future disasters, many aid agencies are investing in longer-term solutions. Projects include improving irrigation systems, which control the flow of water through channels and other devices. This will allow people to make the best use of valuable water supplies.

Scientists are also developing high-quality seeds that will create more, and better-quality, crops. For example, in Kenya researchers and local farmers have developed a new variety of cassava. Cassava is a good plant to grow in harsh climates with little rainfall. The new variety is resistant to disease and produces more crops more quickly than the traditional plants grown by many Kenyan farmers.

These farmers are transplanting rice seedlings in a field in China. Good irrigation systems are vital for the rice plants to grow.

Where is the food going?

A significant percentage of the world's land that is suitable for growing crops is not used to grow food for people. Many crops go into animal feed or are turned into **biofuels** (fuels made from plants). In 2009 one-quarter of the cereal crop in the United States was used for ethanol, a biofuel that is blended with gasoline to power cars and other vehicles. It is estimated that this crop, mostly maize (corn), would have been enough to feed 330 million people.

The GM debate

Today, it is possible to alter the basic makeup of a plant. This technique is called **genetic modification (GM)**.

Plants can be changed to make them more resistant to diseases or pests. They can also be modified so that they contain more of a certain chemical. For example, in regions where rice is a staple food, children often suffer from a lack of vitamin A. This is because normal rice is low in vitamin A. One solution is a GM crop called golden rice. This has been modified to contain higher than usual amounts of vitamin A.

Supporters of GM crops point to their benefits in feeding the rapidly growing populations of the world. But opponents feel that the risks of altering a plant's genetic makeup are huge—and still largely unknown.

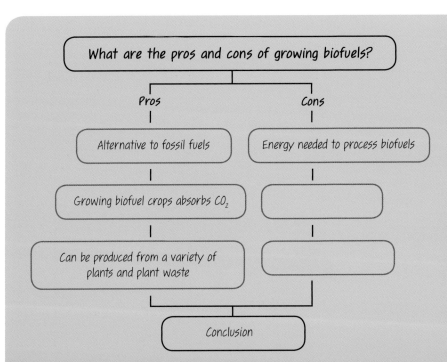

Use a problem-solving box to examine the evidence

Use a problem-solving model to organize facts about complex issues like biofuels.

The top box states the problem. Possible pros and cons are set out in the boxes on the left. The conclusion box shows what you decide about the issue.

Copy and fill in a diagram like this to summarize your research about the pros and cons of biofuels.

WORD BANK

biofuel	fuel that is made from plant matter
genetic modification (GM)	process of altering the genetic makeup of a plant to give that plant certain desirable characteristics
pollution	when the natural world is harmed by waste or by any substance that does not belong there

Water security

Water is essential for growing food, for drinking, for washing, and for cleaning. Yet water is an increasingly precious resource. Worldwide, one in eight people does not have access to water that is safe to drink. Often this is in developing countries with growing populations. Diarrhea, an infection that is passed on through unclean water and causes liquid bowel movements, kills 4,000 children every day.

Like many other resources, water is very unevenly spread around the world. In some countries, water supplies are often very limited. In these places, people (usually women) have to walk many miles every day to fetch clean water. Other countries, such as Bahrain or Kuwait, rely almost entirely on desalination plants, which turn saltwater into freshwater for their supplies.

This map shows projected areas of high water stress in 2025, based on UN figures. It is estimated that more than 2.8 billion people in 48 countries will be short of water by that date.

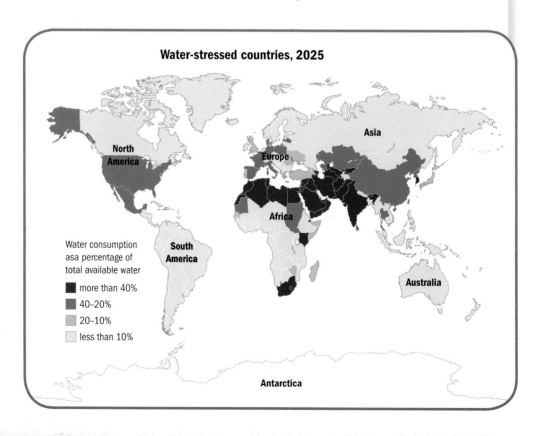

Water-stressed countries, 2025

Water consumption as a percentage of total available water

- ■ more than 40%
- ■ 40–20%
- ■ 20–10%
- □ less than 10%

Unexpected consequences

Aid workers recently provided safe water for a community in Ethiopia, in Africa. At the same time, researchers gathered information on children's births and deaths in the community both before and after the project. Their **data** revealed some unexpected consequences.

Before there were clean-water taps in their villages, local women spent up to six hours each day fetching water in heavy pots from a source far away. After the installation of clean water, this task was much easier. The researchers found that the women rapidly became more fertile and had more babies.

But they also found that these babies were likely to be malnourished, meaning they suffered from lack of good food. This was possibly because limited amounts of food were being shared among larger families. The researchers argued that **contraceptive** advice and improved health care must be carefully considered and offered alongside such projects, in order for everyone involved to truly benefit.

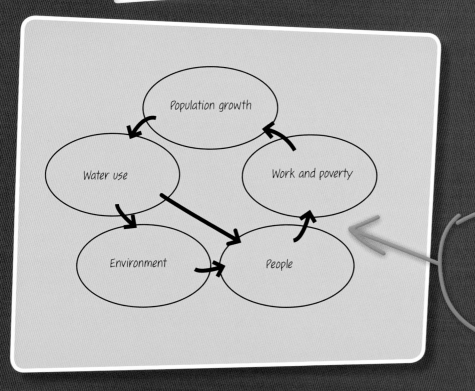

This diagram shows the relationship between population and water use.

Somewhere to Live

As the world fills up with people, finding room for everyone to live is a challenge. In **rural** areas of many **developing countries**, children (usually boys) were traditionally given a share of their parents' land, where they farmed and raised their own families. But increasingly large families have meant that the land has been divided into smaller and smaller pieces.

This is an example of the type of pressure on land that has driven millions of people worldwide to move away from their rural communities into towns and cities, a trend known as **urbanization**. For the first time in human history, in 2008 more than half of the world's population lived in towns and cities. It is predicted that by 2030 this number will grow to almost five billion, with the highest levels of urbanization in Africa and Asia.

Looking for evidence

Do some research to learn more about urbanization, **urban** communities, and family planning projects. Here are some good places to start:

- www.homeless-international.org/Home_1.aspx?id=0:907
- www.raiseinitiative.org/library/factsheets.php

A shantytown in Manila, in the Philippines. Lack of suitable land forces poor urban dwellers to live in dilapidated homes built over the water.

Poverty and urbanization

People move to cities for many reasons—to look for new opportunities and work, to escape rural poverty, and because they are forced to flee their communities as a result of conflict.

Many cities have been overwhelmed by the rapid increases in their populations. New **migrants** often have little choice but to build basic shelters on land around the edges of a city. These communities are known as squatter settlements or **shantytowns**. They are usually built without permission, and most have no access to services such as clean water or **sanitation** (services such as clean water supplies and the removal of **sewage**). The **UN** estimates that around one billion people live in urban slums such as these.

In many cities, squatter communities have formed their own organizations to improve their living conditions. The priorities are to provide safe housing and basic services, such as clean water and sanitation. But **family planning** services are also crucial in helping people in urban slums to move out of poverty.

CASE STUDY

Mobile health brigades

The South American country of Colombia has suffered from years of fighting between armed groups, as well as kidnappings and drug-related violence. Many people have been forced out of their homes, and many move from rural areas to live in the slums of the country's towns and cities.

An organization called Profamilia runs the Mobile Health Brigades Project, which takes family planning and other health services to the places where they are needed. The organization has set up over 40 clinics in the poorest areas of Colombia's cities. Its workers also travel by truck or on foot to remote rural areas. They take medical supplies with them, as well as information about family planning.

WORD BANK

migrant	person who moves from one country or region to another
sanitation	services to provide clean drinking water and to remove sewage
shantytown	slum area, often on the outskirts of a town or city
urbanization	process of migration from rural areas to towns or cities

Cities: Good or bad?

What impact do the massive numbers of people living in cities have on the environment? People live much closer together in cities than they do in rural areas.

Some people believe that this high **population density** (see below) may be good for the environment. This is because public transportation systems can move people around efficiently. Also, water and other services can be more easily provided than in rural areas, where people are more spread out. But others point out that people in cities tend to live lifestyles in which they consume a lot. They say that cities use up large amounts of resources and produce enormous amounts of waste and **pollution**.

Population densities

The number of people living in a particular area is called the population density. It is usually measured as the number of people per square kilometer or per square mile. Averaged across the whole world, the population density is 51 people per square kilometer (132 people per square mile).

But there is a wide variation among different countries. For example, the population density of the United States is 33 people per square kilometer (85 people per square mile), while India's is 369 people per square kilometer (956 people per square mile).

People crowd around fruit and vegetable stalls on the busy streets of Mumbai, India.

Curitiba

Curitiba, in Brazil, South America, is one of the world's best examples of how bold ideas can be put into action to make a city more environmentally friendly—and to give the people who live there a better quality of life. The city has a cheap and efficient public transportation system. People pay the same fare no matter how far they are traveling.

In the 1980s, the city was one of the first to introduce a recycling program for its waste. The city's planners also realized the important role "green spaces" play for the health and well-being of the people who live there. Many of the city's parks have been reclaimed from former industrial sites or wasteland.

One park lies on land that was once a *favela* (shantytown) packed tight with squatters' homes. The land where the squatters lived flooded every year during the rainy season. Today, the area is a park, which has a lake to control the flooding and sheep to graze the grass. The city's planners built low-cost housing for the squatters, located away from the areas that flood.

Today, more than 60 percent of all journeys in the city of Curitiba are by bus.

Environmental impact

Around the world, environments are under threat from the pressures placed on them by the human population. These pressures tend to be greatest where population density is highest.

Coastal regions are one example. Today, around half of the world's population lives within 200 kilometers (125 miles) of a coastline. Average population densities along coastlines are roughly twice the world average, but this figure is considerably higher in urban areas—for example, in Shanghai, China, or in the mega-city of Tokyo in Japan. Many coastal cities are growing fast, as huge numbers of people migrate to these urban areas every year.

The key environmental issues caused by this human impact are:

- *Destruction of **habitats** (natural environments):* Around coastlines, vulnerable habitats can include marshes, beaches, dunes, coral reefs, and trees and shrub called **mangroves**.

- *Pollution:* Air pollution is caused by vehicle **emissions**, while the pollution of coastal waters is caused by sewage or waste from factories and shipping.

- *Resources:* Around coasts, many fish species (types of fish) are in danger from overfishing by modern fishing fleets.

- *Biodiversity (variety of plant and animal life):* The destruction of coastal and marine habitats threatens the wide range of species that live there.

- ***Climate change**:* The major threat to low-lying coasts comes from any future rise in sea level due to climate change.

Parts of the mangrove forests along this stretch of coastline in Borneo, Malaysia, have been cleared to make way for prawn farms.

Palawan Island

Palawan Island, in the Philippines, is a beautiful island that is heavily forested and filled with wildlife in the waters around its white, sandy beaches. It has areas of mangroves as well as large coral reefs along its coasts. In 2000 it had a population of around 750,000, but this population is predicted to double in less than 30 years.

Palawan Island's wildlife and environment are already under threat from human activity—for example, from increased fishing around its coasts.

The World Wildlife Fund (WWF) led a project that focused on health and family planning in areas, like Palawan Island, where the environment and natural resources were most threatened. The group worked with local communities to train volunteers to talk to couples about the links between population, health, and the environment. One of the most important messages was that controlling family size allows parents to provide for their children, while not hurting the environment. In addition to this service, the WWF and local village governments ensured that supplies of **contraceptives** were available at low cost to those who wanted and needed them.

The beautiful scenery of Palawan Island in the Philippines.

WORD BANK
habitat   natural environment of an animal or plant
mangrove   type of tree or shrub that grows along tropical coastlines in marshes and swamps

37

Planning for the Future

*"Preventing unwanted pregnancies in **developing countries** through **family planning** might be one of the most cost-effective ways to preserve the environment."*

UNFPA Family Planning and the Environment

If birth rates were to stay at the same level we have today, by 2050 the world's population would reach 11.9 billion. As it is, experts predict that the rate will slow down, thanks to the increasing use of **contraceptives**. Population growth will, however, be concentrated in the world's **developing countries**, and specifically among the poorest populations of **urban** areas.

In **developed countries** and fast-developing countries such as China, India, and Brazil, birth rates have already stabilized. In many developed countries, birth rates have fallen to below **replacement level**. The **UN** estimates the replacement level to be 2.1 children per woman. This means that the populations of some countries, including Germany, Italy, and Japan, are expected to be lower in 2050 than they are today.

A grandmother hugs her granddaughter in Japan. Japan is one of the countries predicted to have a lower population by 2025 than today.

Migration

Migration will play an important part in any consideration of population issues in the future. Some **migrants** move from one place to another within their own countries—the most common pattern being a move from **rural** to urban areas (see pages 32 and 33). Some are **refugees** from wars and other conflicts. Many others cross borders in search of work and new opportunities.

In 2005 around 191 million people lived outside their home country. Around half of these people were women. Large numbers of migrants send money back to support family in their home countries. This is an extremely important source of income for people in many developing countries.

Migration is likely to increase in future years. Because of the high rates of population growth in many developing countries, millions of young people are entering the workforce. Many of these people cannot find work at home, so they will look beyond the borders of their country. At the same time, developed countries will need migrant workers to fill some of the gaps left by their aging populations (see page 15).

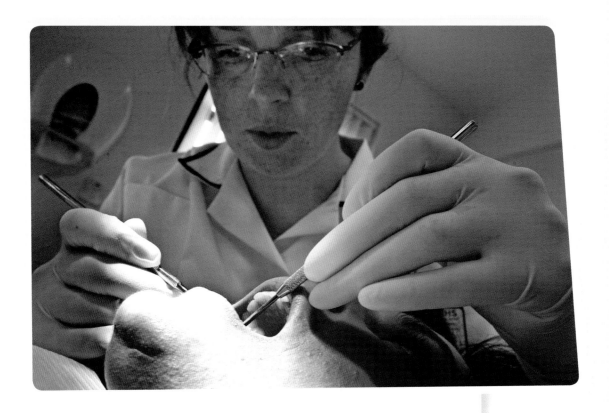

A Polish dentist does a routine check at a hospital in Scotland. Many developed countries will increasingly rely on migrant workers to keep vital services going.

Poverty and education

There is a lot of evidence to show that efforts to slow population growth and invest in education, particularly for women, result in a reduction in poverty. Families with fewer children are better able to feed, educate, and care for each child.

Women who have fewer pregnancies are also more likely to be able to complete their education and to work. Girls who continue their education, and often go on to work, are also more likely to delay the age of their first pregnancy—another important factor in reducing the number of children per woman.

A female teacher with a class of girls at a school in Pakistan. Education for girls has many beneficial effects.

A sustainable future?

How can we create a **sustainable** world, meaning one in which we do not damage the environment for future generations? Some of the biggest challenges for the future lie in developing countries. If population growth is slowed in these countries, people will have more time to take measures to protect their fragile environments and to meet the needs of their populations.

But people in developed countries have a large part to play, too. While population growth in these countries is stable, people in the developed world are major consumers and polluters. It is essential that people in developed countries start to consume and pollute less—and to recycle more. These measures are necessary for the future well-being of all children, in every part of the world.

This wind farm in the United States produces electricity that is fed into the area's grid to power homes and industry.

"The wealthiest countries, with less than 20 percent of Earth's population and the slowest population growth, account for 86 percent of natural resource **consumption**— much of it wasteful—and produce the majority of the **pollution** and **carbon dioxide**."

UNFPA

CASE STUDY

Soap opera studies

Television can be a powerful tool in the battle to slow population growth. In Mexico, soap operas known as *telenovelas* were watched by millions of people on the national television network in the 1970s and 1980s. The shows contained dramatic storylines that illustrated the importance of issues such as **literacy** and contraception. In the decade following a show that dealt with contraception, the country's birth rate dropped by 34 percent. Other countries have since borrowed this technique, with similar exciting melodramas on both radio and television.

WORD BANK
carbon dioxide   colorless gas we breathe out, made of oxygen and carbon
nutrition   food that is necessary for health and growth
sustainable   describes something that happens without damaging the environment for future generations

Fact File: Developing Countries and Developed Countries

Developing countries

"Developing country" is a term used to describe a poor country with a low standard of living. Another term for the poorest countries in the world is "Least Developed Country" (LDC). The **UN** looks at various indicators to decide whether or not a country falls into this category. They include:

- average income per person

- **nutrition** and problems with malnutrition (lack of nutrition)

- health and the **under-five mortality rate**

- number of children receiving an education

- number of adults who are able to read and write (**literacy** rate)

- size of the population

- economy

- number of homeless people.

According to the UN, in 2009 there were 49 developing countries, or LDCs—33 in Africa, 15 in Asia, plus Haiti in the Caribbean. You can look at the full list and find out more about all these countries at www.unohrlls.org/en/ldc/related/62/.

Developing country population facts at a glance

The following are some quick facts about developing countries:

- Population growth is centered in these countries.

- Population growth is slowing thanks to increased use of **contraceptives**.

- Populations have a high percentage of young people.

- Populations do not use many resources.

- Populations do not cause many **carbon dioxide emissions**.

Developed countries

"Developed country" is a term that is used to describe a wealthy country with a high standard of living. Another term for the wealthiest countries in the world is "More Developed Country" (MDC).

According to Kofi Annan, former secretary general of the UN, "A developed country is one that allows all its citizens to enjoy a free and healthy life in a safe environment." This category covers North America, Europe, Australia and New Zealand, Japan and Singapore, and several Middle Eastern countries.

Developed country population facts at a glance

The following are some quick facts about developed countries:

- Population growth is stabilized and, in some cases, negative.
- Populations have a high percentage of older people.
- Populations use a lot of resources.
- Populations cause a lot of carbon dioxide emissions.

Glossary

biofuel fuel that is made from plant matter

carbon dioxide colorless gas we breathe out, made of oxygen and carbon

census official count of everyone living and working in a particular country or region at a particular time

climate change change in the temperature, rainfall, or wind of a region

consumption buying and using things

contraceptive device or drug that is used to prevent pregnancy

data collection of facts

developed country wealthy country where people have a high standard of living

developing country poor country where people do not have a high standard of living

drought long period without rain

ecological footprint measure of the impact of each person on the planet's resources. It is also called the global footprint.

economist expert in economics (the study of money and how it works)

emission release of a gas

family planning planning how many children to have, and when to have them, often through the use of contraceptives

fertile capable of reproducing. The word is used to describe having babies, as well as land that is capable of growing a lot of crops.

genetic modification (GM) process of altering the genetic makeup of a plant to give that plant certain desirable characteristics

global footprint see "ecological footprint"

global warming worldwide rise in the surface temperature of Earth, believed by most experts to be caused by human actions

habitat natural environment of an animal or a plant

HIV/AIDS Human Immunodeficiency Virus (HIV) is a virus that attacks the body's immune system. Acquired Immune Deficiency Syndrome (AIDS) is caused by HIV. As the immune system gradually stops working, sufferers have no defense against infections—they become "immune deficient." There is no cure for HIV, although there are drugs that can help to slow down its progress.

import bring something in from an outside source

life expectancy average number of years people from a certain place live

literacy ability to read and write

mangrove type of tree or shrub that grows along tropical coastlines in marshes and swamps

migrant person who moves from one country or region to another

migration movement of people

natural increase difference between the number of births and deaths in a particular place

nonrenewable something that cannot be replaced once it runs out

nutrition food that is necessary for health and growth

pollution when the natural world is harmed by waste or by any substance that does not belong there

population density number of people per square kilometer or per square mile in a particular place

refugee person who is forced to leave his or her home as a result of war or natural disaster

renewable something that can be replaced naturally, and therefore cannot run out

replacement level number of births that will keep the population stable from one generation to the next

rural from the countryside

sanitation services to provide clean drinking water and to remove sewage

sewage dirty water from toilets, baths, and sinks

shantytown slum area, often on the outskirts of a town or city

sustainable describes something that happens without damaging the environment for future generations

under-five mortality rate number of babies who die before their fifth birthdays

United Nations (UN) organization of different countries that formed in 1945 to promote world peace and security

urban from the city

urbanization process of migration from rural areas to towns or cities

vaccination technique of giving a person a tiny amount of a disease (the vaccine) to give the person protection against the disease in the future

Find Out More

Books

Bellamy, Rufus. *Population Growth (Sustaining Our Environment)*. Mankato, Minn.: Amicus, 2011.

Etingoff, Kim. *Population Growth and Health (Health and the Environment)*. New York: Alphahouse, 2009.

Jakab, Cheryl. *Sustainable Cities (Global Issues)*. Mankato, Minn.: Smart Apple Media, 2010.

Mcleish, Ewan. *Can the Earth Survive? Population Explosion*. New York: Rosen, 2010.

Orr, Tamra. *Counting Our People (21st Century Skills Library)*. Ann Arbor: Cherry Lake, 2010.

Snedden, Robert. *The Growth of Cities (Earth's Changing Landscape)*. Mankato, Minn.: Smart Apple Media, 2005.

Wirkner, Linda. *Learning About Urban Growth in America with Graphic Organizers.*New York: PowerKids, 2005.

Websites

www.wateraid.org
WaterAid is an international organization. It uses practical solutions to provide clean water, safe sanitation, and hygiene education to the world's poorest people.

www.unfpa.org/public/home
The United Nations Population Fund (UNFPA) website offers lots of information about all aspects of population growth.

www.un.org/popin/index.html
The United Nations Information Network website gives you access to the latest UN statistics about populations.

www.prb.org
The Population Reference Bureau provides information about population, health, and the environment.

www.mariestopes.org
The mission statement of Marie Stopes is "Children by choice not chance." Find out more about the work of this organization on this website.

www.raiseinitiative.org
"RAISE" stands for "Reproductive Health Access, Information and Services in Emergencies." This organization is committed to providing family planning and health services to refugees and other people in emergency situations.

www.worldwildlife.org/what/communityaction/index.html
Check out the "Community Action" section of the World Wildlife Fund (WWF) website. You will find out how the WWF is putting family planning at the heart of many of its projects.

www.sierraclub.org/population/
The Sierra Club fosters "healthy communities by advancing sustainable development solutions."

www.footprintnetwork.org/en/index.php/GFN/
The Global Footprint Network website gives more details about footprint science and measuring your own global footprint.

www.census.gov
Find out about the U.S. Census at the U.S. Census Bureau website.

Further research

"Wind turbines, solar (Sun) power, wave power . . . all of these technologies are important for the future. But the 'greenest' of all technologies is contraception."

Think about this statement. Using information from the websites above, find out why family planning could be one of the best ways to reduce carbon dioxide emissions and to tackle global warming.

Index